A-MAZE-ING ADVENTURES

A-MAZE-ING ADVENTURES AMONG THE STARS

Lisa Regan

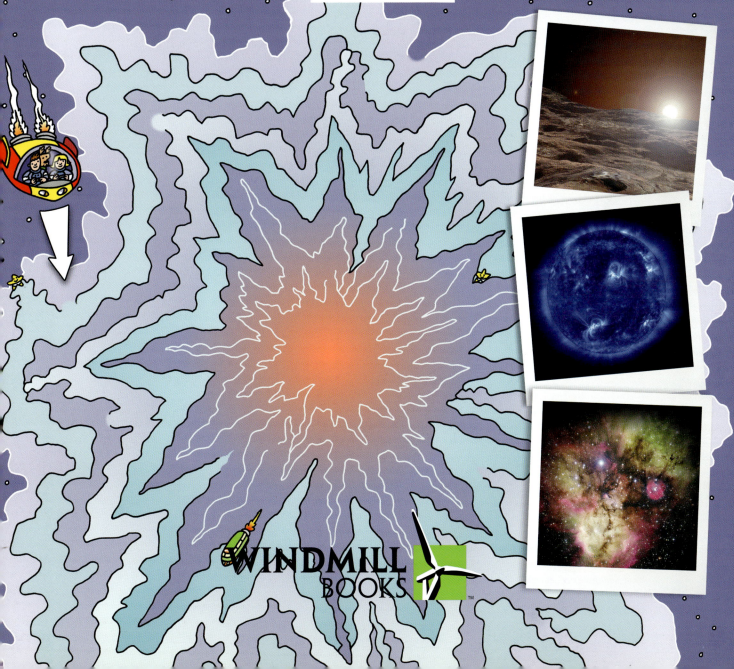

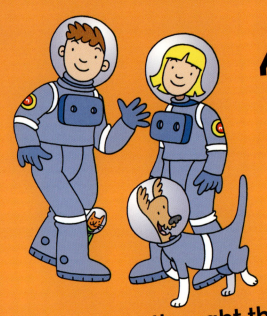

ARE YOU READY TO JOIN US ON AN AMAZING SPACE ADVENTURE?

Who'd have thought that we—Max, Millie, and our pet dog, Mojo—would get the chance to explore space? Along the way, we'll need your help. Use your finger to get through these fun mazes, while looking for hidden objects. As we go, we'll find out lots of fascinating facts! There's so much to explore, so let's get going. 3-2-1... blast off!

Published in 2021 by Windmill Books,
an Imprint of Rosen Publishing
29 East 21st Street, New York, NY 10010

Copyright © Arcturus Holdings Ltd, 2021

Cataloging-in-Publication Data

Names: Regan, Lisa.
Title: A-maze-ing adventures among the stars / Lisa Regan.
Description: New York : Windmill Books, 2021. | Series: A-maze-ing adventures | Includes glossary and index.
Identifiers: ISBN 9781499485578 (pbk.) | ISBN 9781499485592 (library bound) | ISBN 9781499485585 (6 pack) | ISBN 9781499485608 (ebook)
Subjects: LCSH: Maze puzzles--Juvenile literature. | Stars--Juvenile literature.
Classification: LCC GV1507.M3 P484 2021 | DDC 793.73'8--dc23

All rights reserved. No part of this book may be reproduced in any form without permission in writing from the publisher, except by a reviewer.

Manufactured in the United States of America

CPSIA Compliance Information: Batch BS20WM: For Further Information contact Rosen Publishing, New York, New York at 1-800-237-9932

Find us on

Contents

Space Adventure	4
Starry Starry Night	6
All Aboard	8
Up and Away	10
Life in Space	12
Space Walk	14
To the Moon	16
Over the Moon	18
Star Factories	20
A Star Is Born	22
Dying Stars	24
What Remains	26
Answers	28
Glossary	30
Further Information	31
Index	32

Ted the ginger cat has stowed away on our trip. See if you can find him in each maze... He's very shy, so he likes to find some sneaky hiding places!

SPACE ADVENTURE

It all starts one starry night while we're camping. The night sky looks amazing through our telescope, and we can see all sorts of exciting things. We weren't expecting to see aliens, though! Luckily for us, our encounter is with a group of friendly beings from outer space who offer to show us the sights. Our first stop is Earth's moon, and we learn some handy tips about space travel along the way.

START

EARTH

FINISH

MOON

Our alien tour guides want to teach us about the life and death of stars, so they're taking us around the Milky Way galaxy. It's a great place to show us where stars are made, and what happens when they burn out and die. So, if you've ever wanted to see stars up close, now's your chance...

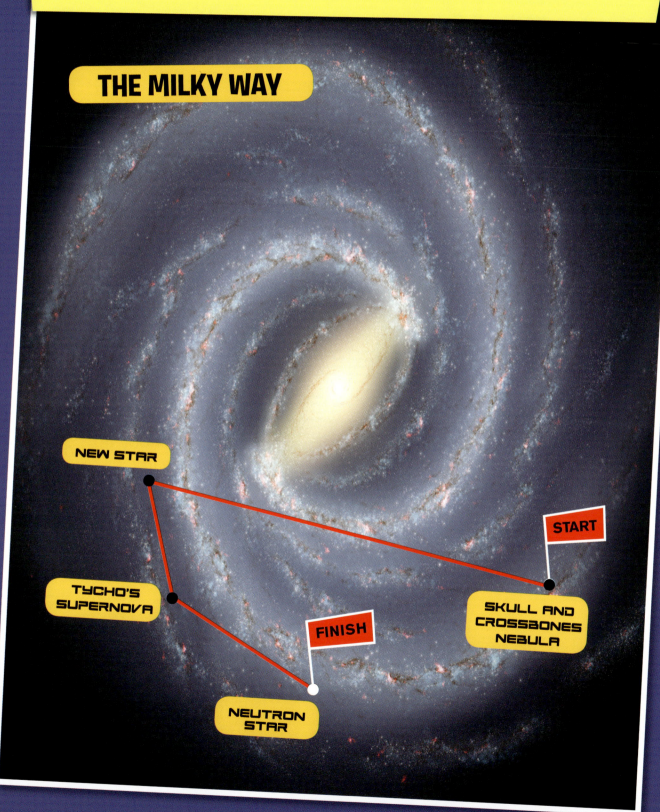

THE MILKY WAY

STARRY STARRY NIGHT

A camping trip gives us the perfect opportunity to check out the stars above us.

FACT FILE
NAME: Earth
NEAREST STAR: the sun
DISTANCE FROM SUN: 93 million miles (150 million km)

It's easy to see some stars without a telescope, and on a clear night, you can pick out patterns of stars, called constellations. Look through a telescope, though, and you will see much more. Astronomers use very powerful instruments to study the universe. The Paranal Observatory in Chile (shown here) uses lasers to pinpoint objects in the sky. Its four telescopes can see things that are four billion times fainter than the human eye can see!

The Paranal Observatory is nicknamed the VLT – Very Large Telescope!

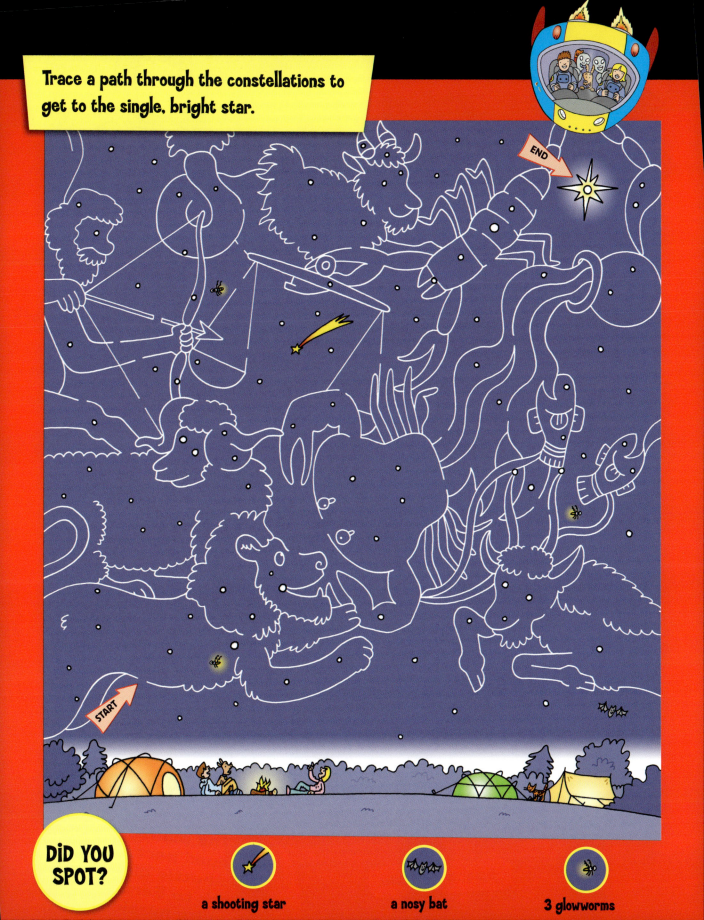

ALL ABOARD

We're about to join a very special group – the select few people who have journeyed into space. Less than 600 men and women have rocketed away from Earth!

FACT FILE

NAME: Earth
LENGTH OF DAY: 24 hours
LENGTH OF YEAR: 365 days

The first space missions in the 1950s had no people on them. Then, in 1961, Soviet cosmonaut Yuri Gagarin became the first person to visit space. Early spacecraft could be used only once. However, in 1981, the U.S. launched the space shuttle, the first reusable spacecraft. It was blasted skyward by large rocket boosters, which detached before the craft reached space.

space shuttle

The plane-shaped part of the shuttle glided back to Earth after its mission, allowing it to be used again.

Max, Millie, and Mojo will need space suits. Help them up to the control room to get ready.

END

START

DID YOU SPOT?

the space spider
the galactic goldfish
the teddy bear

UP AND AWAY

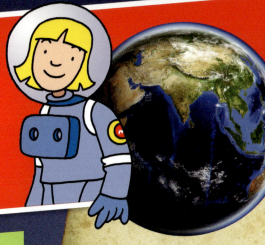

We're ready for liftoff. The rocket is about to blast us off Earth and above its atmosphere. Fasten your seat belts for the ride of a lifetime!

FACT FILE
NAME: Earth
ATMOSPHERE: 280 miles (480 km) thick, made mostly of nitrogen

The atmosphere appears on satellite images as a fuzzy blue circle.

Our planet is surrounded by a blanket of gases called the atmosphere, which acts as a protective layer from the sun's harmful rays. It helps to keep the planet at the right temperature to support life. This is one of the reasons why Earth is the only inhabited planet that we know of. Weather occurs in the lowest layer, the troposphere. The outer layer, the exosphere, is where "outer space" begins.

Spacecraft speed up as they get higher in the atmosphere.

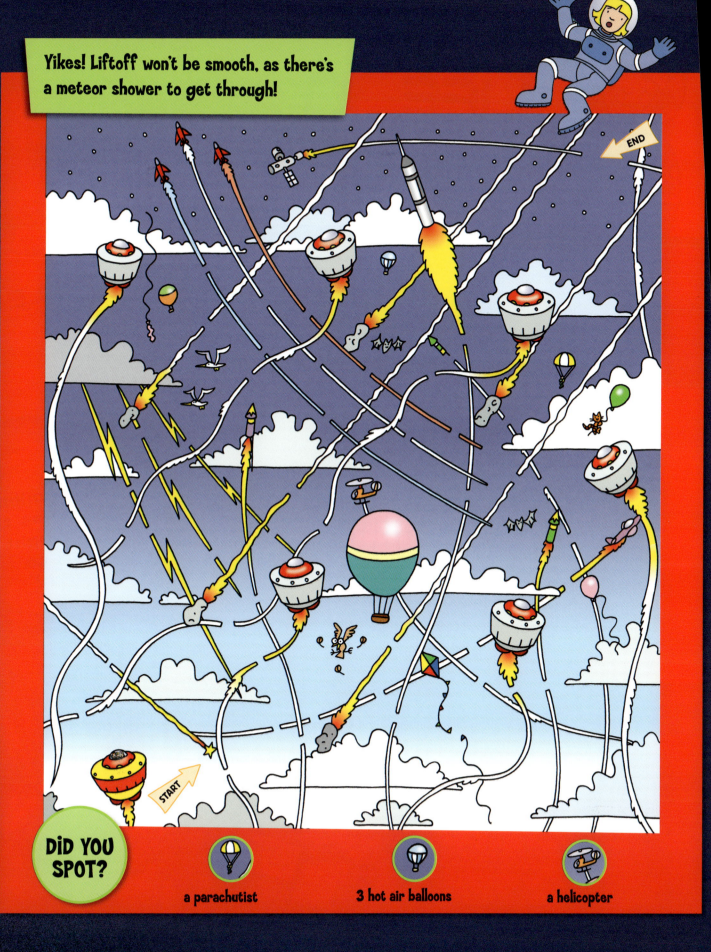

LIFE IN SPACE

It's stange being inside a spaceship. It's easy to float around and turn somersaults in midair! The food looks very different too...

FACT FILE
NAME: Earth
SIZE: four times larger than the moon

Astronauts train for hundreds of hours to prepare for life in space. They learn to operate complicated equipment and cope with the effects of weightlessness. Everything has to be fastened down so it doesn't float around. Even eating food is different. The containers have to be strapped to a tray with fabric fasteners. Astronauts must do lots of exercise every day to keep their muscles from getting weak.

Solid toilet waste has to be brought back to Earth!

Ted the cat is looking for somewhere to hide. Help him find a safe place in the engine room.

DID YOU SPOT?

the alien mouse

the mug of toxic tea

the big red button

Space food often needs to be mixed with water.

Astronauts throw away their dirty clothes instead of washing them.

SPACE WALK

Who would have thought it? We're about to go for our first space walk – Mojo too! We have special suits to protect us outside the spaceship.

FACT FILE

NAME: space walk
ALSO KNOWN AS: EVA (extravehicular activity)

These days, astronauts can live in space for months at a time. They stay on the International Space Station (ISS), which can be seen orbiting Earth in the night sky. It contains six laboratories for research, plus living areas for up to seven astronauts. It was built in space from separate parts carried up on spacecraft (including the space shuttle). Astronauts made around 160 space walks to put the parts together.

The ISS is the largest human-made thing in space.

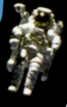

This astronaut is using a special backpack to move around in space.

Help us through the maze to mend the broken wires at the top!

DID YOU SPOT?

 3 space barnacles

 the repair robot

 the space wrench

TO THE MOON

Now we're heading to the moon! Earth's moon is the fifth largest in the solar system. It is the only natural body that orbits Earth.

FACT FILE

NAME: the moon
DISTANCE FROM EARTH: 238,600 miles (384,400 km)

In order to reach the moon, spacecraft need to break free of Earth's gravity. The first mission to do this was Apollo 8 in 1968. A huge rocket blasted three astronauts into space. A smaller craft called the Command and Service Module (or CSM) then detached and continued to the moon. The astronauts took amazing photos of their view of Earth and circled the moon 10 times.

The cockpit of a spacecraft is very complicated.

Uh-oh! The engine doesn't sound right. Help Mojo wriggle through to fix the problem.

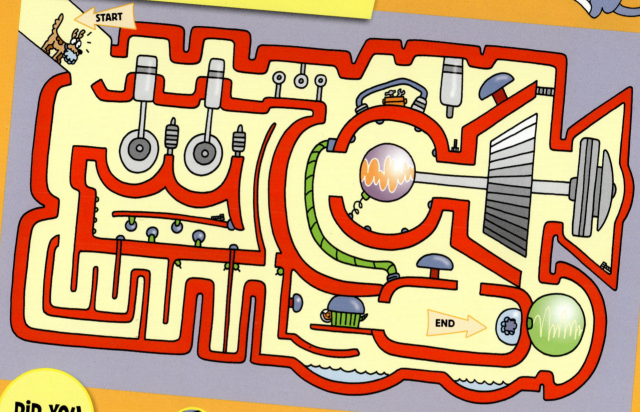

DID YOU SPOT?

a toolbox

3 bolts

4 hubs

The voyage to the moon was in the CSM (Command and Service Module).

Dark areas called seas on the moon's surface can be seen from Earth.

OVER THE MOON

We have landed! We're following in the footsteps of the famous Apollo 11 mission that first put people on the moon in 1969.

FACT FILE

NAME: the moon
ORBIT TIME: 27.3 days to orbit Earth
SIZE: 2,159 miles (3,475 km) across

On July 20, 1969, a lunar module touched down on the surface of the moon for the very first time. It contained U.S. astronauts Neil Armstrong and Buzz Aldrin. A third astronaut, Michael Collins, stayed in orbit in the CSM, waiting to carry them home. The men walked on the moon's surface and collected rock samples to study back on Earth.

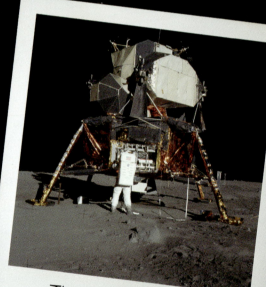

The lunar module was called the Eagle.

Later missions took wheeled vehicles called lunar rovers to the moon.

We're here! Help Max, Millie, and Mojo learn to moonwalk from start to finish.

DID YOU SPOT?
- the ball
- the terrifying tentacle
- the chunk of moon cheese

STAR FACTORIES

It may look like we're steering into a storm, but it's actually a nebula, where new stars are made!

FACT FILE

NAME: Horsehead Nebula
WHAT IS IT? dust/gas clouds
DISTANCE FROM EARTH: 1,500 light-years

The plural of nebula is nebulae.

Nebulae are enormous clouds of dust and gas, many light-years wide. They are often nicknamed stellar nurseries, as they are the birthplace of new stars. The materials in a nebula are so heavy they collapse on themselves, forming large stars inside the clouds. The Skull and Crossbones Nebula (seen here) is around 15,000 light-years away and contains many young stars that can be seen as bright blue dots.

A STAR IS BORN

So, now that we know what stars are and where they are made, do you want to watch one being born?

FACT FILE
NAME: accretion disk
WHAT IS IT?: spinning disk of material from which a new star is formed

Gravity pulls dust and gas together.

When clouds of dust and gas in a nebula begin to swirl around, they turn into clumps. Stars form when the hydrogen gas in a clump is squeezed so hard by gravity it begins to change into another gas (helium), giving off enormous amounts of light and heat energy (shown here). This creates a new star that can burn and shine. Other clumps may form planets that orbit around the new star.

Most newborn stars lie in the middle of a flat disk of dust.

Steer Max, Millie, and Mojo through this spinning, swirling maze to the newborn star!

DID YOU SPOT?

a blue space worm

a superhero

a sandwich

DYING STARS

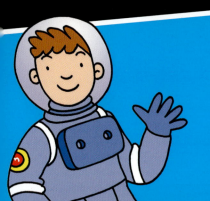

We've watched a star being born. Now we're on our way to see a dying star. Get ready for something spectacular!

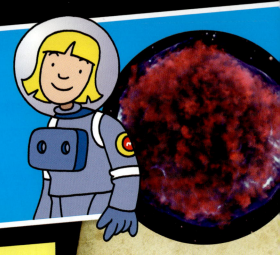

FACT FILE
NAME: Tycho's Supernova
WHAT IS IT?: star explosion
DISTANCE FROM EARTH: 9 light-years (approximately)

All stars have a limited amount of fuel, and when it is all used up, they die. The way a star dies varies depending on its size. Giant stars burn quickly and then expand when they near the end of their life. Finally, they burst apart in an enormous explosion known as a supernova. Tycho's Supernova (pictured below) exploded in 1572 and burned brightly for about a year.

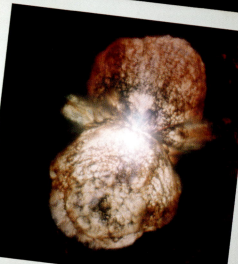

Eta Carinae began to explode in 1843 but is quiet for now.

The bigger a star is, the faster it runs out of fuel.

Watch out for the supernova blast! Find a way out of the middle, as fast as you can!

START

END

DID YOU SPOT?

the space fire truck

the silly scientist

the frazzled fish

WHAT REMAINS

Phew! That was explosive! Now the aliens want to show us what's left after a supernova.

FACT FILE

NAME: neutron star
WHAT IS IT? star remnant
SIZE perhaps just 6 miles (10 km) across

A star doesn't just disappear after a supernova explosion. The outer layers are blown away into space, but the central core is left behind. It no longer burns gas. Instead, it collapses and forms a very small, very dense neutron star. A piece of neutron star the size of a sugar cube would weigh about 100 million tons (90 million metric tons) back on Earth!

Neutron stars spin very fast – as much as 600 times a second!

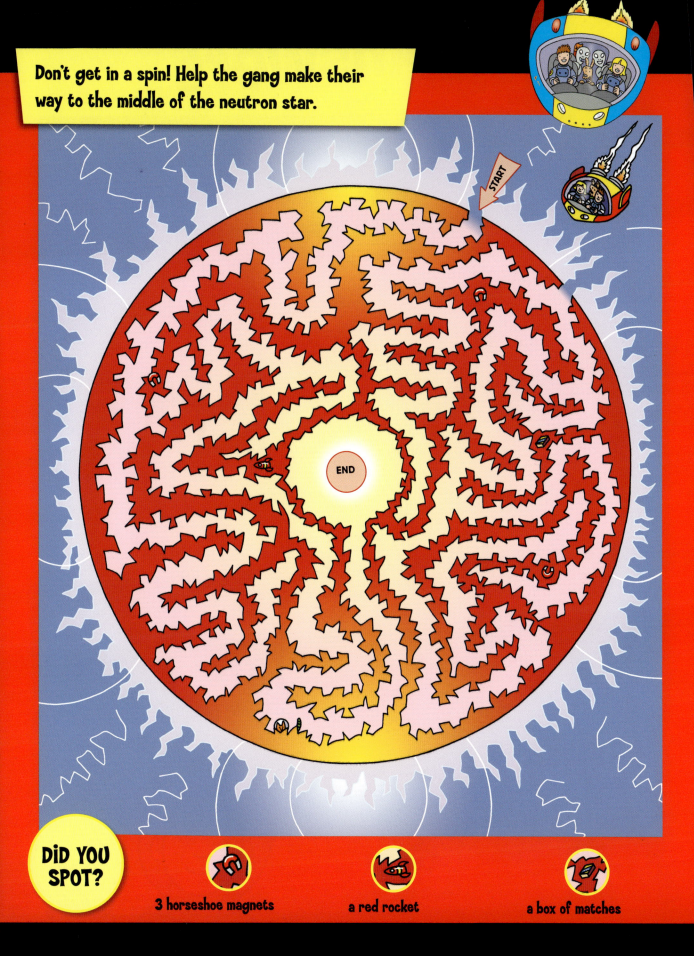

Answers

6–7 Starry Starry Night

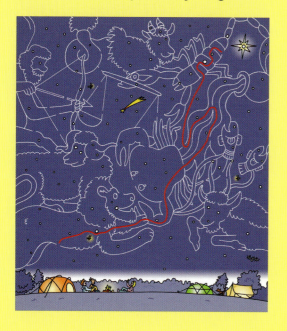

8–9 All Aboard

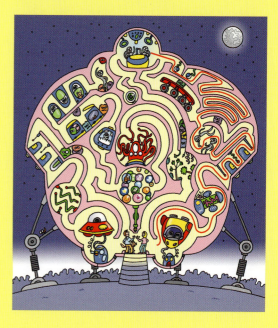

10–11 Up and Away

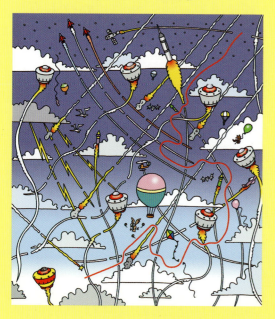

12–13 Life in Space

14–15   Space Walk

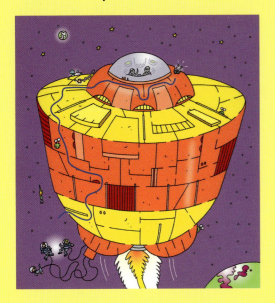

16–17   To the Moon

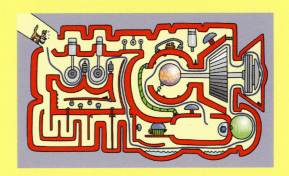

20–21   Star Factories

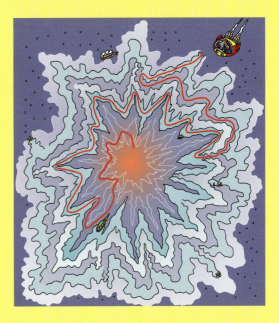

18–19   Over the Moon

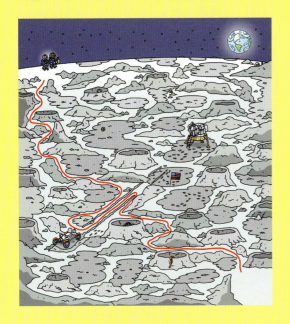

22–23   A Star Is Born

24–25 Dying Stars

26–27 What Remains

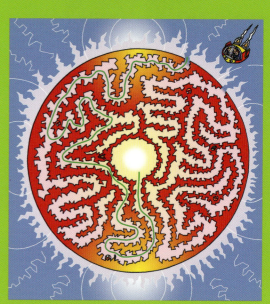

Glossary

astronomer A scientist who studies space and the universe.

atmosphere A layer of gases surrounding Earth or other planets.

cosmonaut A Russian astronaut.

galaxy Millions of stars, gas, and dust in space held together by gravitational force.

gravity The force that pulls all objects in the universe toward each other.

inhabit To live in a place or on a planet.

laser A device that makes a strong, narrow beam of light.

light-year A unit of distance that is the same as the distance light can travel in one year.

meteor A small rock that enters Earth's atmosphere from space.

orbit The curved path of an object in space around a star, planet, or moon.

telescope An instrument that contains lenses arranged to make faraway objects appear closer.

universe The whole of space and all the matter in it.

weightlessness A feeling of weighing nothing when gravity is not acting on the body.

Further Information

Books

A Guide to Space by Kevin Pettman, Wayland, 2019

Imagine You Were There: Walking on the Moon by Caryn Jenner, Kingfisher, 2019

The First Man on the Moon by Ben Hubbard, Wayland, 2019

The Story of Space by Catherine Barr, Frances Lincoln Children's Books, 2017

WOW Space: A Book of Extraordinary Facts by Raman Prinja, Kingfisher, 2020

Websites

www.esa.int/kids/en/home

Find out about space with the European Space Agency. Their website includes information, news, and things to do.

www.google.com/earth

Explore the world in stunning satellite imagery.

www.nasa.gov/kidsclub/index.html

NASA is the U.S. space agency. Explore space and learn interesting facts with their Kids' Club.

Publisher's note to educators and parents: Our editors have carefully reviewed these websites to ensure that they are suitable for students. Many websites change frequently, however, and we cannot guarantee that a site's future contents will continue to meet our high standards of quality and educational value. Be advised that students should be closely supervised whenever they access the Internet.

Index

Aldrin, Buzz 18
Armstrong, Neil 18
astronauts 12, 14, 16, 18
astronomers 6
atmosphere 10

Collins, Michael 18
constellations 6, 7

Earth 4, 10, 14, 16, 17, 18, 26

food 12, 13

Gagarin, Yuri 8
gravity 16, 22

International Space Station (ISS) 14

Milky Way 5
missions 8, 16
   Apollo 8 16
   Apollo 11 18
   moon 4, 16–17, 18–19

nebula 20
neutron star 5, 26–27

Paranal Observatory, Chile 6

rocket 10
rovers 18

Skull and Crossbones Nebula 5, 20
solar system 16
spacecraft 8, 16
spaceship 12, 14
space shuttle 8, 14
stars 5, 6, 7, 20–21, 22–23, 24–25
sun 10
supernova 24, 25, 26
   Eta Carinae 24
   Tycho's Supernova 5, 24–25

universe 6

weightlessness 12